Heartbeat Poetry

Arya Telang

BookLeaf
Publishing

India | USA | UK

Presentation by *BookLeaf Publishing*

Web: www.bookleafpub.com

E-mail: info@bookleafpub.com

ISBN: 978-93-5744-449-1

First edition 2022

Pond

I feel his skin ripple under my touch,
smooth like the water until
my finger skids across the surface
and I hear him moan
in love, lust, longing.
Begging me to continue, but in contradiction
His hand comes up to stop mine from moving
down,
a gentle smile and glazed eyes, erratic breathing
and
a hesitancy to act upon his feelings.
So I stop until the ripples
seize and the
water stills.

Morning

I open my eyes to the feel of the sun upon my
face
except -
It's his radiant smile I wake to.
His figure curved towards me in a protective
embrace
as he whispers, "My love, dream of me."
My ears strain to hear the birds
chirping outside the window
except -
It's his soothing voice murmuring sweet
nothings
that float away with the wind,
and I'm left alone in bed, cold sheets and regrets
embracing me
restrictively.
This is what I wake to
first thing in the morning.

Envy

I envy the love one feels
while my heart sits against the stone-cold floor
in reprieve and punishment
for breaking his heart.
Metal bars hinder me from touching
the warmth of your soul.
And I profusely apologize
for taking your heart away
as my own.
I envy the love one feels
because I can feel that no more.
And I know
neither can you.

Moments

I live in the moments when our fingertips brush
and the hairs on my arm stand up
from desire, not unease,
from yearning, not a passing breeze.
I live for the sole purpose of feeling
You against my skin,
my heart against your chest
and your head by my neck
where my shoulder meets my windpipe
because you are the reason for my every breath.
Proximity does more than our words ever will,
because even if I do not meet you again
You are more than a passing moment
locked away in the back of my mind.
So savor this feeling
and I beg of you, please,
Please just stay the night.

Beat

I fight you with harsh words and poison-laced
remarks
to stir you up and see the evident rage in your
eyes
blaze forth like an untamed beast
in all of its horrifying glory.
There's a pleasure in seeing
the fire behind your pupils
as an exhilarating ride
because I know you will use your hands and I
want
to see you fully
let go.
I want to see you
throw the glass and
smash your fist
against the wall and
see the rash decisions
You will make
under the influence of alcohol.
But don't you dare
lay a hand on me.
I am not yours to touch
in that way.

Memories

I fall too fast and too far into
Your mind
to see that the ground is inches
from my face
and the reality of your death
leaves me broken in more places
than a simple fall from a building
full of memories.
Our memories.

House

I play house with you
like a broken record on repeat
that won't stop singing
"You're a failure, a cheat."
I play house with you
since I do not know
any other games
to keep me entertained.
But are we more than figurines
at the mercy of a greater being?
And is our house more than a symbol of love
built from stones of hurt and trust?
Or do we play house
to distract ourselves
from the impending end of
our fun and games, our turns of phrase?
I play house with you
like I love you.
But you don't play fair,
and when you come home late at night,
I stare at the ceiling
and wish -
I wish I was the winner in your eyes.

Kisses

I ask you to kiss me -
to reach for my lips,
to wrap your arms around my waist,
to hold me in your loving embrace.
I ask you to kiss me -
but you do not care to
Listen.
You never
Listened -
to my requests
to my conquests
to my success.
You never kissed me
Goodbye.

Guard

I feel my breath catch in my windpipe
and choke on the air that's too slow to go
through my mouth and down my throat,
into my lungs and back out slowly.
Because your dimpled cheeks and soft smile
caught me off guard,
and now I can't think straight
or remember the last time
I tilted my head
and kissed you
and told you
how cute you looked.
Because your raised brows and crinkled eyes
caught me off guard,
and now I can't think straight
or remember the last time
I smiled back.
Until your hand brushes against mine,
and my muscle memory is jolted to life.
Because touching you feels like electricity,
Our wires tangled in comforting mutuality.

Monologue

I tried to start my monologue
with something other than "I" -
maybe "we" instead,
but you won't know
how wrong it felt
to go on
when this is no longer
about you.
Even if I've moved on,
You're still here
like a scar that fades but
sticks and stays and
stains and sways and -
I watch you from above
like a guardian angel
that can never say a word.
Your gentle smile
pressed upon my skin,
I wish to take your hand,
but you - you must still live.

Stability

You and I, the tears in my eyes,
lingering fears that slowly subside
like the foam on the surface of the ocean
because this relationship only seems calm
on top, but underneath it all,
It's a fighting typhoon - anything but stable.
Even in your arms, I'm afraid of falling
to my knees and seeing
the rest of me, broken and bruised,
purplish hues,
hammered into my heart from a forgotten past.
Just promise me
you'll provide me with
love and life, and
some simple stability.

Pieces I

I see the remnants of my heart
lying on the ground.
I watch you bend down
on your knees and move around,
until all the pieces of you and I
are found.
You pick up each shard
as if the glass isn't cutting into your skin
and drawing crimson blood
that taints a bleeding heart -
like you've found all the pieces
and there's not a single shard
gone missing.
You hold it as it reflects the light;
You tell me it looks prettier this way,
and I foolishly believe you
that my heart should stay cracked halfway.
It's better broken in your hands than
stored in some casket faraway.

Pieces II

You try to fix something
that wasn't meant to be broken
in the first place.
You pick up the pieces and
connect them as if
Our love could hold it
Together in the same way
I wrap tape around the two ventricles
and glue together each tube of the aorta
and sew the gap between the two atriums.
But the cracks grow and the blood resurfaces,
so the beauty is lost when I see
the remnants of my trusting heart.

Realization

I ask, "How can I love again,
when I'm still in love
with the man who left me
all those years ago?"
This brand new feeling was fulfilling
and fleeting,
but watching you stand right here
in front of me
made me say in fear,
"Don't act like the past hasn't changed
the way you feel about me
because I can't say the same
when you turn to look at me."
I ask you to stop staring at me
with your broken eyes
glassy eyes
diamond-studded teary eyes
that have shattered at the realization
that this is unrequited love.

Stars

I wish upon
the whole of the universe
because a single star
is not enough
to bring you back
to earth.

Quilt

Will you be able to sew me together
like a patched-up quilt
full of memories and arguments?
When we tear, we split at the seams
but forget that we're still whole
and made from the same string.
This quilt of ours under which
I've fallen asleep with
your arm tucked under my head
your hand on my waist
your breath against my ear
your head nestled by my clavicle
your leg resting on top of mine,
Our spines curved in design under
the quilt I am now folding up.

Rope

I climb this mountain on a rainy day
with my feet slipping off the slick edge
where the rocks waste away.
My hands fumble with the small crevices
where I had once lost what is
the reason for my being.
Where I had once lost
You
as
You
fell.
I wish the rope around my waist
had been tied somewhere else
as I feel the wiry brown fibers
graze against my palms,
watching the blood well and wash away
with the rivulets of rain.
The threads dig into the skin
on the inside of my right wrist,
a wrist you'd kissed
when you first saw
Me.

Moonlight

I am a lover of the sun
who shuns and burns me
time and time again.
But I can't disappear for long
because I need you
so that I can shine as if
I'm worth the silver to your gold.
I am a guardian angel
that follows your movement in
admiration, waxing and waning
while I watch with you,
and you look
for me.

Tides

I am the tide that
changes by day and whispers by night,
moving in and out, near and far,
undeciding in my sweeping movements
as I wash away what we used to be.
You stand and watch, but don't move
from your place, rooted in reality
like dreams that can't fly away.
Eyes searching for harmony,
but we are too out of sync
to wish away the pain,
to mend what dissolves
in the salty water we call our tears.
You wonder where we went wrong
but maybe we were never
right for each other,
I say, seeing your chest
falling and rising in sync
with mine.

Race

When you ran off, I ran to you.

I ran to you so hard and so fast I could feel my calf muscles clenching the same way my heart clenched every time I saw you.

I ran like a demon was running after me, fear beating against the walls of my chest like it was a wooden drum, the cover strained, tightly held together, ready to tear the same way it tore when I saw you again.

The beat kept me in sync, pumping blood and making me feel alive, more alive than I had ever felt with you.

I ran to you like rivers run to oceans and stars orbit in motion, like deer run across fields and knights run for shields.

I ran to you.

I ran to you like lovers run to each other in fields of flowers, wind billowing in their hair and smiles plastered onto their faces, except I couldn't see your face because you were turned away from me; you were running away from me.

I ran to you like the moon follows the sun in desperation, hoping to be noticed but only ends up a mere reflection of her lover and wastes away day after day because sometimes opposites don't attract.

I ran to you.

And you ran too.

But you ran too fast, too far, too hard, too much. Until you were a small speck on the horizon, long gone, gone, gone.

I ran to you, only later to realize I was running behind, following your footsteps, lost in your shadows, not making a path of my own.

I ran to you until I realized that - sometimes it's not worth fighting for something that isn't meant to be.

And yet, I ran to you. No, I chased you. Like a lioness chases her prey and a hawk eyes her young, I chased you.

Like dogs chase cats and boys chase girls and cops chase robbers and the monster under your bed chases away your dreams because when was the last time anyone ever followed their heart over their head?

In this race of life, I ran and I chased. You ran and you ran until your legs gave out and you fell to the ground as victory was mine and you were nothing more than a small speck on the horizon, meaningless and devoid of the exhilaration and anticipation I provide. Of the adrenaline and oxytocin, magical realism and mystical surrealism -

When I come for you again, you better run. Run like the wind, oh you better run.

Love

I think most people forget that
Love isn't pure, ideological, compatible –
a perfect fit of two halves that align with the
stars.
It's a hole you've dug for yourself deep in the
ground,
but you can't decide whether to climb out
or to stay and turn it around.

It's a single sound that penetrates your ears
and rings eternally, fades but stays, like a
forgotten memory.

It's a struggle between sacrifice and indulgence,
A test of patience and just how much judgment
Is tolerable, acceptable, sensible.

I think most people forget that
Love isn't a declaration with roses and rings –
a compromise between two hearts and two souls
eternally bound by societal strings.

It's a brown paper bag with a mysterious lunch
But no matter what it is, you know you'll eat it

Because inside, there's a note and food made
with love.

I think most people forget that
Love isn't all glitter and gold
nor is it bitter and old –
a cross between the starting passion and ending
depression.

It's a continuing determination to be good
enough
Merely, truly, just you enough.

It's the sad but sincere smile after a fight,
The talking that starts very late at night,
The whirlpool of water where you're being
sucked in
but it's a necessity that has kept you floating
and from drowning alone.

But then again, everyone has a different
definition of love,
and maybe that's simply lovely –
how it's so flexible, incomprehensible, mildly
bearable.

I think most people forget that
Love does exist, whether it be in
the darkest corners or the brightest places,

the struggles that show your investment –
a mountain that you've prepared to climb,
but a high you do not want to come down from.

I think most people forget that.

www.ingramcontent.com/pod-product-compliance
Lightning Source LLC
LaVergne TN
LVHW041300200726
843507LV00014B/3072